Edited by
Bart Tesoriero

Illustrations by
Michael Adams

Nihil Obstat:	Reverend Francis Vivona, S.T.M., J.C.L.
Imprimatur:	Most Reverend Bishop William C. Skurla, D.D., Bishop of the Eparchy of Van Nuys
Date:	June 6, 2007

Scripture excerpts are taken from the *New American Bible with Revised New Testament and Psalms*
Copyright © 1991, 1986, 1970 Confraternity of Christian Doctrine, Inc., Washington, DC.
Used with permission. All rights reserved. No part of the *New American Bible* may be reproduced
by any means without permission in writing from the copyright holder.

Library of Congress Control Number: 2011909350
ISBN 1-61796-055-0

Copyright ©2007, 2012 by Aquinas Press
First Edition, 2007; Second Edition, 2012
Sixth Printing, December, 2012

TABLE OF CONTENTS

Fatherhood	5
Counsels and Maxims for Married Men	6
A Rule of Life for Catholic Men	8
A Brief Statement of Catholic Doctrine	10
Morning Prayers	16
Prayers for Every Day	18
Prayer to Saint Michael the Archangel/Spiritual Armor	23
Evening Prayers	24
Prayers Before Communion	28
Prayers After Communion	30
Prayer Before a Crucifix	33
Prayer to the Blessed Virgin	35
Litany of the Most Holy Name of Jesus	36
Devotions to the Holy Name of Jesus	39
Act of Consecration to the Sacred Heart of Jesus	43
Litany of the Sacred Heart of Jesus	44
Family Prayers to the Sacred Heart of Jesus	46
Act of Spiritual Communion	47
Devotions to the Holy Spirit	48
How to Pray the Rosary	50
The Joyful Mysteries of the Rosary	52
The Luminous Mysteries of the Rosary	54
The Sorrowful Mysteries of the Rosary	56
The Glorious Mysteries of the Rosary	58
Consecration to the Hearts of Jesus and Mary	60
A House Blessing	60
Prayer for Our Marriage	61
Prayer to Conceive	62
Thanksgiving for Conceiving	63

Prayer for a Happy Delivery	64
Prayer for My Wife After Childbirth	65
Blessing of an Infant/Blessing of a Child	66
Blessing of a Family/Family Prayer	67
Prayer for a Handicapped Child	68
Prayer for a Sick Child	69
Prayer for a Growing Infant	70
Prayer for My Children	71
Child Correction	72
For the Grace to Properly Correct a Child	73
For a True Spirit of Fatherhood	74
Prayer for Strength	75
Prayer After a Miscarriage	76
Prayer at the Death of a Child/Prayer to a Child in Heaven	77
Dedication of a Family to Mary	78
Thanksgiving for a Happy Family	79
For Protection of the Family	80
For True Family Prosperity	81
For the Grace to be Faithful to Our Marriage	82
For a Child in Moral Danger	83
For a Wayward Son	84
For a Wayward Daughter	85
For a Son or Daughter Considering Marriage	86
For a Married Son or Daughter	87
Prayer for Healing/Prayer For a Sick Wife	88
Prayer for a Deceased Wife	89
Litany of Saint Joseph	90
Novena to Saint Joseph	93
Scriptures for Fathers	Inside Back Cover

FATHERHOOD

King Solomon wrote, "A wise son makes his father glad." (PROVERBS 10:1) But how does a father make a wise son? Fatherhood is a gift, a vocation, a challenge, a delight, and a cross, all rolled into one. Fatherhood is an invitation to love!

God calls a husband to love his wife with a devoted, tender, and fervent love that prefers her to all others. The vocation of a father, along with his wife, is to lead his family to heaven. Parents have the duty to love and respect their children as persons and as the children of God, and to provide, as far as possible, for their physical and spiritual needs. The Church calls parents to educate their children in the ways of the Lord and to help them discover and fulfill God's designs for them. Parents do this mainly through their example, shared prayer, teaching, and their own participation in the life of the Church.

We are providing this Manual to help fathers grow in their own relationship with God, *their* Father! We have included maxims, a summary of Catholic teaching, daily prayers, litanies, novenas, and devotions. We also provide a section on how to pray the Rosary, with brief meditations on all 20 mysteries, as well as prayers about marriage, children, family, and healing, and end with scriptures for fathers.

Take a moment today and spend it with Our Lord! We pray that you will feel God's love in your heart and His presence in your life, for your good and the good of your family, in your all-important vocation of building on earth His Kingdom of love.

COUNSELS AND MAXIMS FOR MARRIED MEN

Husbands, love your wives, even as Christ loved the church and handed himself over for her.
—Ephesians 5:25

- A husband should strive to continue after marriage the manly chivalry, strength, generosity, and tenderness that made him so attractive in the days of his courtship.

- Reverence is the product of the home, and what is learned in the home is never forgotten.

- The unselfish husband will never be unmindful of the great burdens and sacrifices which marriage and motherhood lay upon a woman.

- After marriage your wife should come first in your affections, but this does not mean that you are to neglect your mother or father, whom you can never repay for all they have done for you.

- Parents may advise, but should never force upon their children any particular career in life.

- The best thing a father can do for his children is to love their mother.

- The light that shines furthest shines brightest at home.

- A loving soul illumines and warms the house better than a blazing hearth and a lighted lamp.

- The married who live in harmony and mutual love can defy the world; without this unity, all the world cannot make them happy.

- The best way to win the respect and obedience of your children is to show them good example.

- A father who neglects prayer, Mass, and the Sacraments, must never wonder when his children do likewise.

- The father is the head, the mother the heart of the home.

- Mutual consideration and tolerance are sure to make married life happy.

- You cannot have the respect of your children if you disrespect their mother.

- Children bring blessings to every good home, and they are one of the surest guarantees of the unity and fidelity of the husband and wife.

- And at all times remember your vows:
  I, *(name)* take thee, *(name)* for my lawful wife,
  to have and to hold, from this day forward,
  for better, for worse, for richer, for poorer,
  in sickness and in health, until death do us part.
  Amen.

A RULE OF LIFE FOR CATHOLIC MEN

Every Day

1. Begin and end each day with prayer, and pray at some time during the day.

2. Try to spend at least a few moments each day in serious spiritual reflection, preferably reading the Scriptures, lives of the saints, or devout books, even if just a few sentences.

3. Be faithful to all daily duties, in or out of the home.

4. When possible, attend Mass during the week and make a regular visit to the Blessed Sacrament.

5. Give focused attention to your wife and children.

6. Every evening, make a simple review of your day. Thank God for your successes; ask His forgiveness for your failures; and request His grace to improve a bit tomorrow.

Every Week

7. Always attend Sunday Mass, if possible with your family. Make Sunday a special day to worship the Lord and to share true leisure with family and friends. If possible, reach out to others in need, especially the sick or elderly.

Every Month

8. Go to Confession at least once a month, and make a good examination of your conscience.

9. Tithe to the Lord
   "Bring the whole tithe
      into the storehouse,
   That there may be food in my house,
      and try me in this, says the LORD of hosts:
   Shall I not open for you the floodgates of heaven,
      to pour down blessing upon you without measure?"
   —MALACHI 3:10

Every Year

10. Set aside a few days of your time each year to attend a retreat; and always make the mission with your parish.

Often

11. Make it a habit to frequently deny yourself some luxury, and give to the poor and worthy causes as you are able.

Always

12. Avoid indecent or uncharitable talk and conversations.

13. Avoid all persons, places, TV programs, internet sites, and books that are dangerous to morals or a waste of time.

A BRIEF STATEMENT OF CATHOLIC DOCTRINE

The Ten Commandments of God— Exodus 20:1-17

1. I am the Lord your God. You shall not have strange gods before Me.

2. You shall not take the name of the Lord your God in vain.

3. Keep holy the Sabbath.

4. Honor your father and your mother.

5. You shall not kill.

6. You shall not commit adultery.

7. You shall not steal.

8. You shall not bear false witness against your neighbor.

9. You shall not covet your neighbor's spouse.

10. You shall not covet your neighbor's goods.

The Seven Deadly Sins

Pride	Humility
Covetousness	Generosity
Lust	Chastity
Anger	Meekness
Gluttony	Temperance
Envy	Brotherly Love
Sloth	Diligence

Contrasting Virtues

Ways of Being Accessory to Another's Sin

- By counsel
- By command
- By consent
- By provocation
- By praise or flattery
- By concealment
- By partaking
- By silence
- By defense of the wrong done.

The Precepts of the Church

1. You shall attend Mass on Sundays and on holy days of obligation, and refrain from doing unnecessary work.
2. You shall confess your sins at least once a year.
3. You shall receive the sacrament of the Eucharist at least during the Easter season.
4. You shall observe the prescribed days of fasting and abstinence established by the Church.
5. You shall help to provide for the needs of the Church.

The Seven Sacraments

Baptism	Matthew 28:19
Eucharist	Matthew 26:26
Reconciliation	John 20:23
Confirmation	Acts 8:17
Matrimony	Matthew 19:6
Holy Orders	Luke 22:19
Anointing of the Sick	James 5:14-15

The Three Theological Virtues

- Faith
- Hope
- Charity

The Four Cardinal Virtues

- Prudence
- Justice
- Fortitude
- Temperance

The Seven Gifts of the Holy Spirit
Isaiah 11:2-3

- Wisdom
- Understanding
- Counsel
- Fortitude
- Knowledge
- Piety
- Fear of the Lord

The Twelve Fruits of the Holy Spirit

- Love
- Joy
- Peace
- Patience
- Kindness
- Goodness
- Generosity
- Gentleness
- Faithfulness
- Modesty
- Self-control
- Chastity

The Corporal Works of Mercy

- To feed the hungry
- To give drink to the thirsty
- To clothe the naked
- To shelter the homeless
- To visit the sick
- To visit the imprisoned
- To bury the dead

The Spiritual Works of Mercy

- To counsel the doubtful
- To instruct the ignorant
- To admonish sinners
- To comfort the afflicted
- To forgive offenses
- To bear wrongs patiently
- To pray for the living and the dead

The Four Last Things

1. Death
2. Judgement
3. Hell
4. Heaven

The Beatitudes

- Blessed are the poor in spirit, for theirs is the kingdom of heaven.

- Blessed are they who mourn, for they will be comforted.

- Blessed are the meek, for they will inherit the land.

- Blessed are they who hunger and thirst for righteousness, for they will be satisfied.

- Blessed are the merciful, for they will be shown mercy.

- Blessed are the clean of heart, for they will see God.

- Blessed are the peacemakers, for they will be called children of God.

- Blessed are they who are persecuted for the sake of righteousness, for theirs is the kingdom of heaven.

- Blessed are you when they insult you and persecute you and utter every kind of evil against you (falsely) because of me. Rejoice and be glad, for your reward will be great in heaven. Thus they persecuted the prophets who were before you.

—Matthew 5:1-13

MORNING PRAYERS

Morning prayers should include adoration of God in His divine majesty, thanksgiving for His protection during the night, and consecration of the day to His service.

On awakening, make the Sign of the Cross ✚, *and pray:*

In the Name of our Lord Jesus Christ crucified, I arise. May He bless my work, govern my every action and preserve me from harm this day.

Kneeling down put yourself in the presence of God, Who loves you:
Free my mind, O Lord, from all distracting thoughts, and enable me to pray at all times with attention and devotion, so that I may deserve to be heard by You. I offer You my prayers in union with the divine intention with which Jesus Himself, while on earth, offered praise to You.

Acts of Adoration

Blessed be the holy and undivided Trinity, now and forevermore. Unto the King of ages, the immortal, invisible, and only God, be honor and glory forever and ever.

I thank You, O my Father, for the innumerable favors and benefits which I have received from Your loving kindness and mercy, especially for having preserved me this night. Glory be to the Father Who has created me; Glory be to the Son Who has redeemed me; and Glory be to the Holy Spirit Who sanctifies me.

Morning Offering to the Sacred Heart of Jesus

O Jesus, through the Immaculate Heart of Mary, I offer You my prayers, works, joys, and sufferings of this day, in union with the Holy Sacrifice of the Mass offered throughout the world, in reparation for all my sins, for all the intentions of Your Sacred Heart, and in particular for the intentions of our Holy Father. Amen.

Daily Consecration to Mary

O Mary, my Queen and my Mother,
I give myself entirely to you.
And as proof of my filial devotion,
I consecrate to you this day
my eyes, my ears, my mouth, my heart,
my whole being without reserve.
Wherefore, good Mother,
As I am your own,
Keep me and guard me
As your property and possession. Amen.

A Father's Prayer

Dear Father, help me to love my children no matter what, to encourage them and to lead them on the right way today. Help me to share my faith in simple, down-to-earth ways, and to let them know I believe in them. Help me to listen with my heart, to lead by my example, and to love them forever. In Jesus' name. Amen.

PRAYERS FOR EVERY DAY

The Sign of the Cross

In the name of the Father, ✠ and of the Son, and of the Holy Spirit. Amen.

The Lord's Prayer

Our Father, Who art in heaven, hallowed be Thy name. Thy kingdom come, Thy will be done, on earth as it is in heaven. Give us this day our daily bread; and forgive us our trespasses, as we forgive those who trespass against us; and lead us not into temptation, but deliver us from evil. Amen.

Hail Mary

Hail Mary, full of grace, the Lord is with thee. Blessed art thou among women, and blessed is the fruit of thy womb, Jesus.

Holy Mary, Mother of God, pray for us sinners, now and at the hour of our death. Amen.

Glory Be to the Father

Glory be to the Father, and to the Son, and to the Holy Spirit; as it was in the beginning, is now, and ever shall be, world without end. Amen.

The Apostles' Creed

I believe in God, the Father almighty,
Creator of heaven and earth,
and in Jesus Christ,
His only Son, our Lord.
He was conceived by the Holy Spirit,
and born of the Virgin Mary.
He suffered under Pontius Pilate, was crucified, died and was buried.
He descended into hell.
On the third day He rose again.

He ascended into heaven,
and is seated at the right hand
of God the Father Almighty.
He will come again to judge
the living and the dead.
I believe in the Holy Spirit,
the Holy Catholic Church,
the communion of saints,
the forgiveness of sins,
the resurrection of the body,
and life everlasting. Amen.

Prayer to Your Guardian Angel

O Angel of God, my Guardian dear,
To whom God's love, commits me here;
Ever this day, be at my side,
To light and guard, to rule and guide. Amen.

The Confiteor

I confess to Almighty God, to blessed Mary, ever Virgin, to blessed Michael the Archangel, to blessed John the Baptist, to the Holy Apostles Peter and Paul, and to all the Saints, that I have sinned exceedingly in thought, word, and deed, through my fault, through my fault, through my most grievous fault.

Therefore I beseech blessed Mary, ever Virgin, blessed Michael the Archangel, blessed John the Baptist, the holy Apostles Peter and Paul, and all the Saints, to pray to the Lord our God for me.

May Almighty God have mercy on me, forgive me my sins, and bring me to everlasting life. Amen.

May the Almighty and merciful Lord grant me pardon, absolution, and remission of all my sins. Amen.

Grace Before Meals

Bless us, O Lord, and these Thy gifts,
which we are about to receive from Thy bounty,
through Christ our Lord. Amen.

Grace After Meals

We give Thee thanks, Almighty God,
for these and all Thy benefits, which we have received from Thy bounty, through Christ our Lord. Amen.
May the souls of the faithful departed,
through the mercy of God, rest in peace. Amen.

Act of Faith

O my God, I firmly believe that You are one God in three divine Persons, Father, Son, and Holy Spirit. I believe that Your divine Son became man, died for our sins, and that He will come to judge the living and the dead. I believe these and all the truths which the Holy Catholic Church teaches, because You have revealed them, Who can neither deceive nor be deceived. Amen.

Act of Hope

O my God, relying on Your almighty power and infinite mercy and promises, I hope to obtain pardon of my sins, the help of Your grace, and life everlasting, through the merits of Jesus Christ, my Lord and Redeemer. Amen.

Act of Love

O my God, I love You above all things, with my whole heart and soul, because You are all-good and worthy of all my love. I love my neighbor as myself for the love of You. I forgive all who have injured me, and ask pardon of all whom I have injured. Amen.

The Angelus

V- The Angel of the Lord declared unto Mary.
R- And she conceived by the Holy Spirit.
(Hail Mary...)
V- Behold the handmaid of the Lord.
R- Be it done unto me according to thy word.
(Hail Mary...)
V- And the Word was made Flesh.
R- And dwelt among us.
(Hail Mary...)
V- Pray for us, O Holy Mother of God.
R- That we may be made worthy of the promises of Christ.

Let us pray: Pour forth, we beseech Thee, O Lord, Thy grace into our hearts; that we to whom the Incarnation of Christ, Thy Son, was made known by the message of an Angel, may by His Passion and Cross, be brought to the glory of His Resurrection. Through the same Christ our Lord. Amen.

The Memorare

Remember, O most gracious Virgin Mary, that never was it known, that anyone who fled to thy protection, implored thy help, or sought thy intercession, was left unaided. Inspired by this confidence, I fly unto thee, O Virgin of virgins my Mother; to thee do I come, before thee I stand, sinful and sorrowful. O Mother of the Word Incarnate, despise not my petitions, but in thy mercy hear and answer me. Amen.

Prayer to Saint Michael

Saint Michael, the Archangel, defend us in battle. Be our safeguard against the wickedness and snares of the devil. May God rebuke him, we humbly pray; and do you, O Prince of the heavenly host, by the power of God cast into hell Satan and all the evil spirits who wander through the world seeking the ruin of souls. Amen.

Spiritual Armor Prayer
Based on Ephesians 6:13-17

Heavenly Father, we ask You today for Your truth as a belt tight around our loins. We put on the zeal to announce Your good news of peace as shoes for our feet. We put on Your righteousness, O Christ, as our breastplate, and the hope of salvation as a helmet for our head. Father, we take up faith as a shield which is able to put out all the fiery darts of the enemy, and the sword of the Spirit, which is Your Word, O Lord. Father, may the love with which You have loved Jesus be in us, and may Jesus be in us. We ask You for the grace of a servant heart. In Jesus' name. Amen.

EVENING PRAYERS

Never neglect your night prayers. Whenever possible, pray with your family. Offer up fervent supplication that you may be protected from harm while you rest. In truth, we never know when Our Lord will come for us. Each night may be our last.

The Sign of the Cross

In the name of the Father, ✠ and of the Son, and of the Holy Spirit. Amen.

Act of Thanksgiving

I most heartily thank You, O Lord, for all Your mercies and blessings which You have given to me, my family, and Your whole Church this day. I particularly thank You for watching over us and preserving us from so many evils, and for favoring us with so many graces and inspirations. *(Here pause and meditate on God's mercies.)*

Oh, let us never be ungrateful to You again, dear God, Who are so good and gracious to us and to all people.

It is good to give thanks to the LORD,
 to sing praise to your name, Most High,
To proclaim your love in the morning,
 your faithfulness in the night,
With the ten-stringed harp,
 with melody upon the lyre.
For you make me jubilant, LORD, by your deeds;
 at the works of your hands I shout for joy.

—Psalm 92:1-4

Examination of Conscience

O my Lord Jesus Christ, Judge of the living and the dead, before Whom I must appear one day to give an exact account of my whole life, please enlighten me and give me a humble and contrite heart, that I may see how I have offended Your infinite Majesty, and that I may judge myself now with a sober judgement, in order that You may judge me then with mercy and compassion.

Here pause a moment and consider where and in what company you have been this day. Call to mind the sins committed against God, your neighbor, or yourself; and reflect on whether you have fulfilled the duties of your state of life.

- **Offenses against God**: Omission or negligence in religious duties; irreverence and willful distractions in prayer; lack of confidence and trust in God; cursing, swearing...

- **Offenses against our neighbor**: Want of obedience or respect; scandal, hatred, quarreling; stealing; injuries; lies, false reports; jealousy, desire of revenge...

- **Offenses against self**: Vanity, human respect; actions, thoughts, desires, or language against purity; intemperance in eating or drinking; laziness and neglect of my duties...

Pray the Confiteor (see page 20).

Act of Contrition

O my God! I am heartily sorry for having offended Thee, and I detest all my sins, because I dread the loss of heaven and the pains of hell, but most of all because they offend Thee, my God, Who art all good and deserving of all my love. I firmly resolve, with the help of Thy grace, to confess my sins, to do penance, and to amend my life. Amen.

Evening Prayer of Saint Augustine

Watch, O Lord, with those who wake,
or watch, or weep tonight,
and give Your Angels and Saints
charge over those who sleep.
Tend Your sick ones, O Lord Christ.
Rest Your weary ones,
Bless Your dying ones,
Soothe Your suffering ones,
Pity Your afflicted ones,
Shield Your joyous ones,
And all for Your love's sake. Amen.

Ancient Prayer to the Virgin Mary

We turn to you for protection, holy Mother of God.
Listen to our prayers, and help us in our needs.
Save us from every danger, O glorious and blessed Virgin.

Prayer for the Faithful Departed

O God, the Creator and Redeemer of all the faithful, grant to the souls of Your departed servants the remission of all their sins, that, through our fervent supplications, they may obtain that pardon which they have always desired. We ask this in the name of Jesus, your Son, Amen.

Night Prayer of Protection

Visit, we beseech You, O Lord, this habitation, and drive far from it all snares of the enemy. Let Your holy angels dwell herein, to preserve us in peace; and may Your blessing be always upon us, through our Lord Jesus Christ.

Save us, O Lord, when we are awake, and keep us while we sleep, that we may watch with Christ, and rest in peace. Amen.

PRAYERS BEFORE HOLY COMMUNION

Preparation for Holy Communion

We should never receive the Holy Eucharist unless we are free from serious sin, and have prepared ourselves well. The benefit we derive from our Communion is in proportion to our devotion and preparation. Jesus wants to bless us with His presence, and we need to be ready for Him.

Prayer of Supplication

Dear God my Heavenly Father, in the name of Jesus Christ Your Son, I come before You. I come as one sick to the Divine Physician, as one unclean to the Source of all mercy, as one blind to the Light of the eternal sun, and as one poor and needy to the Lord of heaven and earth.

I beg of You, from the abundance of Your great love and mercy, to cleanse me from my sins, enlighten my understanding, enrich my poverty, and clothe my nakedness. Allow me to receive Jesus, the Bread of angels, the King of kings, and the Lord of lords, with reverence and humility, contrition and devotion, purity and faith, with integrity of heart and desire of spirit, for the salvation of my immortal soul and the good of my family, friends, and all people. Amen.

Act of Offering

Dear Jesus, I offer myself to You this day as I prepare to receive You in Holy Communion. Please make me ready to receive You with all the love in my heart. Amen.

Abandonment to God

Take my body, Jesus,
Eyes and ears and tongue;
Never let them, Jesus,
Help to do You wrong.

Take my heart and fill it,
Full of love for Thee;
All I have I give Thee,
Give Thyself to me.

Act of Praise

Dear God, I worship You today, Father, Son, and Holy Spirit! Thank You for being my Father and Lover. I praise You for Who You are, Good Shepherd and King of Love. To You be praise, to You be glory, to You be thanksgiving forever and ever! Amen.

My Eucharistic Intention

As I receive You, please grant unto me, O almighty and merciful Lord, joy with peace, amendment of life, space for true repentance, the grace and comfort of Your Holy Spirit, perseverance in good works, a contrite and humble heart, and a happy fulfillment of my life. Amen.

As you go up to receive Communion, pray:

"Jesus, with desire I desire to receive You."

PRAYERS AFTER HOLY COMMUNION

Thanksgiving After Holy Communion

Returning to your seat, reflect on the gift of the Eucharist you have just received—the Body and Blood, Soul and Divinity of Jesus Himself, given because He loves you! Speak to Jesus in your own words, and use the following or other prayers if you so choose.

Prayer After Communion

O Jesus, You have just come to me in Holy Communion.
Your Body is living in my body.
Your Heart is beating in my heart.
You are truly present in me now.
Thank You, Lord Jesus, for coming into my heart.
I need You very much. I need Your strength, I need Your hope,
and I need Your unconditional love.
Please don't ever leave me.
I love You, Jesus.
I want to live forever with You in heaven.
Today I give myself to You—my body, my mind, my heart.
Please keep me and those I love close to Your Heart,
and bring us back to You if ever we stray from You.
Jesus, I love You. Amen.

Anima Christi

Soul of Christ, sanctify me;
Body of Christ, save me;
Blood of Christ, inebriate me;
Water from the side of Christ, wash me;
Passion of Christ, strengthen me;
O good Jesus, hear me;
Within Your wounds, hide me;
Separated from You, let me never be;
From the evil one, protect me;
At the hour of my death, call me;
And close to You, bid me; That with Your saints, I may be,
Praising You forever and ever. Amen.

Prayer Before a Crucifix

Look down upon me,
good and gentle Jesus,
while before Your face I humbly kneel
and, with burning soul,
pray and beseech You,
to fix deep in my heart,
lively sentiments of faith, hope, and charity;
true contrition for my sins,
and a firm purpose of amendment;

While I contemplate,
with great love and tender pity,
Your five most precious wounds,
pondering over them within me
and calling to mind the words
which David, Your prophet,
said of You, my Jesus:

"They have pierced my hands and my feet,
They numbered all my bones."
Amen.

Prayer to the Blessed Virgin

O most holy, noble, and glorious Virgin Mary, God found you worthy to bear in your blessed womb the Creator of all, and at your virginal breast to nourish Him Whose true, real, and most holy Body and Blood I, an unworthy sinner, have just now been privileged to receive. Thank you so much for saying "Yes" to God's Will, and allowing the Son of God to be born through you for all of us.

Dear Mother, Jesus gave you to us on the Cross to be our mother as well. He knew we would need your help in following Him, and He also wanted us to experience the joy He knew in having you for His mother. Jesus wants each of us to be saved and to live forever with Him, His Father, and their Holy Spirit in heaven.

Therefore, with confidence I humbly ask you to intercede with Your Son for me. I entrust to you my wife, my family, and myself with all our hopes and fears. Pray for us that the Holy Spirit would give us the light of true wisdom, and guide our steps in the ways of peace. Help each of us to come to know and love your Son—the Way, the Truth, and the Life.

Sustain us, O Virgin Mary, on our journey of faith and obtain for us the grace of eternal salvation. O clement, O loving, O sweet Mother of God and our Mother, Mary!

We ask this in the name of Jesus Christ, your Son, Who with the Father and the Holy Spirit lives and reigns forever and ever. Amen.

Litany of the Most Holy Name of Jesus

V. Lord, have mercy. R. **Christ, have mercy.**
V. Lord, have mercy.
V. Jesus, hear us. R. **Jesus, graciously hear us.**
V. God the Father of Heaven,
R. **Have mercy on us.**
V. God the Son, Redeemer of the world,
R. **Have mercy on us.**
V. God the Holy Spirit,
R. **Have mercy on us.**
V. Holy Trinity, One God,
R. **Have mercy on us.**

R. **Have mercy on us.**

Jesus, Son of the living God,
Jesus, Splendor of the Father,
Jesus, Brightness of eternal Light,
Jesus, King of Glory,
Jesus, Sun of Justice,
Jesus, Son of the Virgin Mary,
Jesus, most amiable,
Jesus, most admirable,
Jesus, the mighty God,
Jesus, Father of the world to come,
Jesus, Angel of great counsel,
Jesus, most powerful,
Jesus, most patient,
Jesus, most obedient,
Jesus, meek and humble of heart,
Jesus, Lover of Chastity,
Jesus, our Lover,
Jesus, God of Peace,
Jesus, Author of Life,

Jesus, Model of Virtues,
Jesus, zealous for souls,
Jesus, our God,
Jesus, our Refuge,
Jesus, Father of the Poor,
Jesus, Treasure of the Faithful,
Jesus, Good Shepherd,
Jesus, true Light,
Jesus, eternal Wisdom,
Jesus, infinite Goodness,
Jesus, our Way and our Life,
Jesus, **J**oy of the Angels,
Jesus, **K**ing of the Patriarchs,
Jesus, **M**aster of the Apostles,
Jesus, **T**eacher of the Evangelists,
Jesus, **S**trength of Martyrs,
Jesus, **L**ight of Confessors,
Jesus, **P**urity of Virgins,
Jesus, **C**rown of all Saints,

V.	**Be** merciful,	R.	Spare us, O Jesus.
V.	Be merciful,	R.	Graciously hear us, O Jesus!

R. Jesus, deliver us.

From all evil,
From all sin,
From Your wrath,
From the snares of the devil,
From the spirit of fornication,
From everlasting death,
From the neglect of Your inspirations,
Through the mystery of Your Holy Incarnation,
Through Your Nativity,
Through Your Infancy,

R. Jesus, deliver us.

Through Your most divine Life,
Through Your Labors,
Through Your Agony and Passion,
Through Your Cross and dereliction,
Through Your Sufferings,
Through Your Death and Burial,
Through Your Resurrection,
Through Your Ascension,
Through Your Institution of the Most Holy Eucharist,
Through Your Joys,
Through Your Glory,

V. Lamb of God, Who takes away the sins of the world,
R. Spare us, O Jesus!
V. Lamb of God, Who takes away the sins of the world,
R. Graciously hear us, O Jesus!
V. Lamb of God, Who takes away the sins of the world,
R. Have mercy on us, O Jesus!
V. Jesus, hear us.
R. Jesus, graciously hear us.

Let us pray: Lord Jesus Christ, You have said, "Ask and you shall receive; seek and you shall find; knock and it shall be opened to you." Mercifully attend to our supplications, and grant us the grace of Your most divine love, that we may love You with all our hearts, and in all our words and actions, and never cease to praise You.

Grant us, O Lord, to have a perpetual awe and love of Your holy name, for You never fail to govern those whom You establish in Your love. We ask this of You, Who lives and reigns with Your Father and the Holy Spirit, One God, forever and ever. Amen.

DEVOTIONS TO THE HOLY NAME OF JESUS

*"You shall not take the name of the LORD, your God, in vain.
For the LORD will not leave unpunished him
who takes his name in vain."*

—Exodus 20:7

*Because of this, God greatly exalted him
and bestowed on him the name
that is above every name,
that at the name of Jesus
every knee should bend,
of those in heaven and on earth and under the earth,
and every tongue confess that
Jesus Christ is Lord,
to the glory of God the Father.*

—Philippians 2:9-11

Devotion to the Holy Name of Jesus began very early in the Church. Acts 19:17 relates that the name of Jesus was held in "great esteem." Saint Bernardine of Siena (1380-1444) and his followers promoted the veneration of the Name of Jesus in public worship, and today the feast of the Holy Name of Jesus is an optional memorial for January 3rd.

Praise to the Holy Name of Jesus

May the Holy Name of Jesus be infinitely blessed!
May the Holy Name of Jesus be infinitely blessed!
May the Holy Name of Jesus be infinitely blessed!
May the Holy Name of Jesus be infinitely blessed!
May the Holy Name of Jesus be infinitely blessed!

Act of Reparation for Blasphemies Uttered Against the Holy Name

O Jesus, my Savior and Redeemer, Son of the living God, behold, we kneel before You and offer You our reparation. We would make amends for all the blasphemies uttered against Your holy name, for the injuries done to You in the Blessed Sacrament, for the irreverence shown toward Your Immaculate Virgin Mother, and for all the calumnies and slanders spoken against Your spouse, the holy Roman Catholic Church.

O Jesus, You said: "If you ask the Father anything in my name, He will give it to you." We pray to You for all our brothers and sisters who are in danger of sin. Shield them from every temptation to fall away from the true faith; save those who are even now standing on the brink of the abyss; give them light and knowledge of the truth, courage and strength for the conflict with evil, perseverance in faith and great love!

For this do we pray, most merciful Jesus, in Your name, to God the Father, with Whom You live and reign in the unity of the Holy Spirit, world without end. Amen.

> *"Who will not fear you, Lord,*
> *or glorify your name?*
> *For you alone are holy.*
> *All the nations will come*
> *and worship before you,*
> *for your righteous acts have been revealed."*
>
> –Revelation 15:4

O Good Jesus

O Bone Jesu

O Good Jesus, according to Your great mercy, have mercy on me. O most merciful Jesus, by that Precious Blood which You shed for sinners, I beseech You to wash away all my iniquities and to look graciously upon me, a poor and unworthy sinner, as I call upon Your holy Name. Therefore, O Jesus, please save me for Your holy Name's sake. Amen.

The following ancient prayer appears in both the Roman Missal and the Liturgy of the Hours.

Bestow upon us, O Lord, both an abiding reverence for and an abiding love of Your Holy Name. You never fail to govern by Your grace those to whom You teach the depths of Your love. Through Christ our Lord. Amen.

Golden Arrow

This prayer is said to have been revealed by Jesus Himself to a Carmelite Nun of Tours in 1843 as a reparation for blasphemy.

May the most holy, most sacred, most adorable, most mysterious and unutterable Name of God be always praised, blessed, loved, adored, and glorified in heaven, on earth, and under the earth, by all the creatures of God, and by the Sacred Heart of our Lord Jesus Christ in the most Holy Sacrament of the altar. Amen!

ACT OF CONSECRATION TO THE SACRED HEART

Most sweet Jesus, Redeemer of the human race, look down upon us humbly prostrate before You. We are Yours, and Yours we wish to be; but to be more surely united with You, behold each one of us freely consecrates himself today to Your Most Sacred Heart. Many indeed have never known You; many, too, despising Your precepts, have rejected You. Have mercy on them all, most merciful Jesus, and draw them to Your Sacred Heart.

Be King, O Lord, not only of the faithful who have never forsaken You, but also of the prodigal children who have abandoned You; grant that they may quickly return to their Father's house, lest they die of wretchedness and hunger.

Be King of those who are deceived by erroneous opinions, or whom discord keeps aloof, and call them back to the harbor of truth and the unity of faith, so that soon there may be but one flock and one Shepherd.

Grant, O Lord, to Your Church, assurance of freedom and immunity from harm; give tranquility of order to all nations; make the earth resound from pole to pole with one cry: Praise to the divine Heart that wrought our salvation; to Him be glory and honor for ever. Amen.

Sacred Heart of Jesus, may Thy Kingdom come!
Most Sacred Heart of Jesus, I put my trust in Thee.
Jesus, meek and humble of heart, make my heart like unto Thine.

THE LITANY OF
THE SACRED HEART OF JESUS

V- Lord, have mercy. **R- Christ, have mercy.**
V- Lord, have mercy. Christ hear us.
R- Christ, graciously hear us.

V- God, the Father of Heaven, **R- Have mercy on us.**
God, the Son, Redeemer of the world, **R- Have mercy on us.**
God, the Holy Spirit, **R- Have mercy on us.**
Holy Trinity, one God, **R- Have mercy on us.**

R- Have mercy on us.

Heart of Jesus, Son of the Eternal Father,
Heart of Jesus, formed in the womb of the Virgin Mother by the Holy Spirit,
Heart of Jesus, united substantially with the Word of God,
Heart of Jesus, of infinite majesty,
Heart of Jesus, holy temple of God,
Heart of Jesus, tabernacle of the Most High,
Heart of Jesus, house of God and gate of heaven,
Heart of Jesus, glowing furnace of charity,
Heart of Jesus, vessel of justice and love,
Heart of Jesus, full of goodness and love,
Heart of Jesus, abyss of all virtues,
Heart of Jesus, most worthy of all praise,
Heart of Jesus, King and center of all hearts,
Heart of Jesus, in whom are all the treasures of wisdom and knowledge,
Heart of Jesus, in whom dwells all the fullness of the Divinity,
Heart of Jesus, in whom the Father is well pleased,
Heart of Jesus, of whose fullness we have all received,

Heart of Jesus, desire of the everlasting hills,
Heart of Jesus, patient and rich in mercy,
Heart of Jesus, rich to all who invoke Thee,
Heart of Jesus, fount of life and holiness,
Heart of Jesus, propitiation for our sins,
Heart of Jesus, saturated with revilings,
Heart of Jesus, crushed for our iniquities,
Heart of Jesus, made obedient unto death,
Heart of Jesus, pierced with a lance,
Heart of Jesus, source of all consolation,
Heart of Jesus, our life and resurrection,
Heart of Jesus, our peace and reconciliation,
Heart of Jesus, victim for our sins,
Heart of Jesus, salvation of those who hope in Thee,
Heart of Jesus, hope of those who die in Thee,
Heart of Jesus, delight of all saints,

V- Lamb of God, who takes away the sins of the world,
R- Spare us, O Lord.
V- Lamb of God, who takes away the sins of the world,
R- Graciously hear us, O Lord,
V- Lamb of God, who takes away the sins of the world,
R- Have mercy on us.

V- Jesus, meek and humble of Heart.
R- Make our hearts like unto Thine.

Let us pray: Almighty and everlasting God, look upon the Heart of Thy well-beloved Son and upon the acts of praise and satisfaction which He renders unto Thee in the name of sinners; and do Thou, in Thy great goodness, grant pardon to them who seek Thy mercy, in the name of the same Jesus Christ Thy Son, who lives and reigns with Thee, world without end. Amen.

FAMILY PRAYERS TO THE SACRED HEART

Family Prayer to the Sacred Heart

Sacred Heart of Jesus, we entrust our family to You. Look down upon us and reveal to us the treasures of love, goodness, and grace in Your Heart. Forgive our sins and strengthen our hearts, that we may serve You faithfully as You deserve.

Help us to love one another, Lord Jesus. Help us to make room for one another, to be willing to work together. Give us Your love which is patient, and kind, which bears all things, hopes all things, and believes all things. Your love never fails!

These favors we ask for ourselves and for every family in our neighborhood and homeland. Heart of Jesus, pierced by a soldier's lance on Calvary, be our refuge in life and our gateway to Paradise. Amen.

Prayer for All Human Needs

Lord Jesus Christ, Your Heart still cherishes all the redeemed. You are moved to compassion for every human need, as You were in the days when You walked among us on earth.

Aware of Your invitation, "Come to Me," we pray for the afflicted, the sick, the confused, for all broken hearts, and shattered lives. We bring to You all their material, emotional, and spiritual needs as well as our own. By the love that led You to take flesh of the Virgin Mary and dwell among us, we plead for a favorable response to our prayers. Amen.

An Act of Spiritual Communion
by Saint Alphonsus Liguori

My Jesus, I believe that You are present in the Most Holy Sacrament. I love You above all things, and I desire to receive You into my soul. Since I cannot at this moment receive You sacramentally, come at least spiritually into my heart. (Pause).

Dear Jesus, I embrace You as if You were already here and I unite myself wholly to You. Never permit me to be separated from You. Amen.

Pope John Paul II, quoting Saint Teresa of Avila, said, "When you do not receive Communion and you do not attend Mass, you can make a Spiritual Communion, which is a most beneficial practice; by it the love of God will be greatly impressed on you."

Since devotion to the Sacred Heart of Jesus is essentially Eucharistic, the act of uniting ourselves with Him spiritually throughout our day brings consolation and joy to His Sacred Heart, and prepares us to receive Him more devoutly when we do receive the Holy Eucharist at Mass.

An Act of Spiritual Communion, according to any pious formula, is enriched with a *partial indulgence.*

DEVOTIONS TO THE HOLY SPIRIT

Come, Holy Spirit, fill the hearts of Your faithful, and kindle in us the fire of Your divine love.

V. Send forth Your Spirit, and we shall be created.

R. And You shall renew the face of the earth.

Let Us Pray

O God, who by the light of Your Holy Spirit has instructed the hearts of Your faithful, grant us in the same Spirit to be truly wise, and ever to rejoice in His consolation. Through the same Christ, our Lord. Amen.

Act of Consecration to the Holy Spirit

O Holy Spirit, divine Spirit of light and love, I consecrate to You my understanding, heart, and will, my whole being for time and for eternity. May my understanding be always submissive to Your heavenly inspirations, and to the teachings of the Catholic Church, of which You are the infallible guide.

May my heart be ever inflamed with love for God and neighbor. May my will be ever conformed to the divine will, and may my whole life be a faithful imitation of the life and virtues of our Lord and Savior, Jesus Christ, to Whom, with the Father and You, be honor and glory forever. Amen.

A SECRET OF SANCTITY

By Cardinal Mercier

I am going to reveal to you a secret of sanctity and happiness. Every day for five minutes, keep your imagination quiet, shut your eyes to all the things of the senses, and close your ears to all the sounds of earth, so as to be able to withdraw into the sanctuary of your baptized soul, which is the temple of the Holy Spirit, and there speak to that Holy Spirit, saying:

> **O Holy Spirit, soul of my soul,**
> **I adore You.**
> **Enlighten, guide, strengthen, and console me.**
> **Tell me what I ought to do and command me to do it.**
> **I promise to be submissive in everything**
> **that You permit to happen to me.**
> **Only show me what is Your will.**

If you do this, your life will pass happily and serenely. Consolation will abound even in the midst of troubles. Grace will be given in proportion to the trial as well as strength to bear it, bringing you to the gates of Paradise full of merit.

This submission to the Holy Spirit is the Secret of Sanctity.

Praise God!

WHAT IS THE ROSARY?

When we pray, we speak to God, vocally or silently, and listen to Him in our hearts. God wants us to know Him and love Him. In the Rosary we pray to God with Mary, the Mother of Jesus and our spiritual Mother as well. As we pray the prayers of the Rosary, we reflect on certain events, or mysteries, in the lives of Jesus and Mary. The Rosary is divided into four groups of five mysteries each. These are the Joyful, Luminous, Sorrowful, and Glorious mysteries.

As we consider each mystery of the Rosary, we try to imagine what was happening and what God wants to teach us. We want to get to know Him and to learn how He wants us to live. But even more, to pray the Rosary is to hold Mary's hand and let her bring us to Jesus. When we are with Jesus and Mary, we know the peace, love, and joy of God.

How to Pray the Rosary

- Begin by making the Sign of the Cross ✢ and and praying *The Apostles' Creed* while you hold the crucifix.

- Pray one *Our Father* on the first bead, three *Hail Marys* on the next three beads for the virtues of Faith, Hope, and Charity, and finish with a *Glory Be*.

- Announce the first Mystery and meditate on it while praying an *Our Father* on the large bead, ten *Hail Marys* on the smaller beads, and finishing with a *Glory Be*. This is one decade.

- If you wish, add the *Fatima Prayer* after the *Glory Be*: "O my Jesus, forgive us our sins; save us from the fires of Hell. Lead all souls to Heaven, especially those most in need of Your mercy." Continue in this way until all you have prayed all five decades. To finish, pray the *Hail Holy Queen*.

Hail, Holy Queen

Hail, Holy Queen, Mother of Mercy,
Our life, our sweetness, and our hope!
To thee do we cry, poor banished
children of Eve; to thee do we send
up our sighs, mourning and weeping
in this valley of tears. Turn then,
most gracious advocate, thine eyes
of mercy towards us; and after this
our exile, show unto us the blessed
fruit of thy womb, Jesus; O clement,
O loving, O sweet Virgin Mary.

V- Pray for us, O holy mother of God,
R- That we may be made worthy of the promises of Christ.

THE JOYFUL MYSTERIES

Monday, Saturday

THE ANNUNCIATION

Then the angel said to her, "Do not be afraid, Mary, for you have found favor with God. Behold, you will conceive in your womb and bear a son, and you shall name him Jesus."
—Luke 1:30-31

The Angel Gabriel told Mary that God had chosen her from all women to be the Mother of His Son. Mary said 'Yes' to God. Because of this, God could become man, and all people could be saved.

Mary believed and trusted God even when it was hard to understand. She obeyed God knowing He always works everything out for the good.

Dear Mother Mary, help us also say yes to God with a willing heart.

THE VISITATION

When Elizabeth heard Mary's greeting, the infant leaped in her womb, and Elizabeth, filled with the holy Spirit, cried out in a loud voice and said, "Most blessed are you among women, and blessed is the fruit of your womb." —Luke 1:41-42

When Mary heard that her cousin Elizabeth was pregnant, she went quickly to visit and help her. Elizabeth was overjoyed to see Mary.

One of the best ways to make others happy is to visit them. In this way, we help bring the love of Jesus to others, just as Mary brought the love of Jesus to Elizabeth and her unborn child.

Dear Mother Mary, thank you for teaching us to be good to others. Help us always bring them joy, that they will feel the love of Jesus.

THE BIRTH OF JESUS

While they were there, the time came for her to have her child, and she gave birth to her firstborn son. She wrapped him in swaddling clothes and laid him in a manger, because there was no room for them in the inn. —LUKE 2:6-7

Long ago in Bethlehem, Mary gave birth to Jesus and laid him in a manger. The angels sang, "Glory to God in the highest, and peace to His people on earth!"

Dear Mother Mary, help us to feel Jesus' love for us, and to love one another as well.

THE PRESENTATION OF JESUS

"Now, Master, you may let your servant go
  in peace, according to your word,
for my eyes have seen your salvation,
  which you prepared in sight of all the peoples,
a light for revelation to the Gentiles,
  and glory for your people Israel." —LUKE 2:29-32

God promised Simeon that he would not die until he had seen the Messiah.

God always keeps His promises, even when we have to wait a long time.

Dear Mother Mary, help us, like Simeon, trust that God will keep all His promises and bring us His salvation.

THE FINDING OF JESUS

"Why were you looking for me? Did you not know that I must be in my Father's house?" But they did not understand what he said to them. —LUKE 2:49-50

Jesus always did his Father's Will, even when others did not understand. Even so, he returned home with his parents and obeyed them.

Dear Mother Mary, help us to obey God our Father, as Jesus did, and to love Him with all our hearts.

THE LUMINOUS MYSTERIES

Thursday

THE BAPTISM OF JESUS IN THE JORDAN
After all the people had been baptized and Jesus also had been baptized and was praying, heaven was opened and the holy Spirit descended upon him in bodily form like a dove. And a voice came from heaven, "You are my beloved Son; with you I am well pleased." –LUKE 3:21-22

Jesus obeyed his Father always, because he loved Him. Jesus teaches us to always begin our day with prayer, that we also may obey our Heavenly Father.

Dear Mother Mary, it is good to know my Heavenly Father loves me as He loves Jesus. Please pray that I will obey Him as Jesus did.

THE WEDDING AT CANA
And when the headwaiter tasted the water that had become wine ... the headwaiter called the bridegroom and said to him, "Everyone serves good wine first, and then when people have drunk freely, an inferior one; but you have kept the good wine until now." –JOHN 2:9-10

Jesus changed water into wine to serve others. In so doing, he revealed his glory. Mary teaches us in this mystery to do whatever her Son tells us.

Dear Mother Mary, when you asked Him, Jesus changed water into wine and opened the hearts of His followers to faith. Help me also trust in God in all that I do.

JESUS PROCLAIMS GOD'S KINGDOM

After John had been arrested, Jesus came to Galilee proclaiming the gospel of God: "This is the time of fulfillment. The kingdom of God is at hand. Repent, and believe in the gospel."
–MARK 1:14-15

Jesus proclaimed the good news that God was calling all people to come back to Him. We can only change our hearts with God's help.

Dear Mother Mary, help me to hear Jesus in His Word and in the quiet of my heart. Help me to obey Him and to love with His love.

THE TRANSFIGURATION OF JESUS

[Jesus] took Peter, John, and James and went up the mountain to pray. While he was praying, his face changed in appearance and his clothing became dazzling white. ... Then from the cloud came a voice that said, "This is my chosen Son; listen to him." –LUKE 9:28-29, 35

Jesus calls us to be the light of the world. When we obey Jesus, His light shines through us. In this way we bring light to everyone!

Dear Mother Mary, you always let the Lord shine His light in you and in your life. Help me listen to Jesus and let His light shine in my heart.

THE INSTITUTION OF THE EUCHARIST

When the hour came, he ... took the bread, said the blessing, broke it, and gave it to them, saying, "This is my body, which will be given for you; do this in memory of me." And he did the same with the cup after they had eaten, saying, "This cup is the new covenant in my blood, which will be shed for you."
–LUKE 22:14, 19-20

Jesus loved us so much that he gave himself so he could always be with us. May Mary help us always prepare a place for Jesus in our hearts.

Dear Mother Mary, thank you for sharing your Son with us so He could bring us His life. May we always be thankful for the gift of His Body and Blood.

THE SORROWFUL MYSTERIES
Tuesday, Friday

THE AGONY IN THE GARDEN
Then they came to a place called Gethsemane… … and [Jesus] began to be troubled and distressed. —MARK 14:32-33

In the Garden of Gethsemane the night before he died, Jesus' friends fell asleep and he was all alone. He felt afraid, lonely, and very sad. Jesus prayed hard for his Father's help.

Jesus placed all his trust and confidence in his Heavenly Father, as he had his whole life. Even when bad things happen, God will always take care of us.

Dear Mother Mary, please help me to remember Jesus and spend time with Him in prayer.

JESUS IS SCOURGED AT THE PILLAR
So Pilate, wishing to satisfy the crowd, released Barabbas to them and, after he had Jesus scourged, handed him over to be crucified. —MARK 15:15

The soldiers arrested Jesus and put him in prison. Pontius Pilate, who was afraid of the people, ordered the soldiers to whip Jesus even though he had done nothing wrong.

The soldiers hurt Jesus very much. Yet during all this time, Jesus was thinking of us. He offered his suffering so we could someday come to heaven to be with him forever.

Dear Mother Mary, please help me to love others even when they are not kind to me. May Jesus live in my heart today.

JESUS IS CROWNED WITH THORNS

The soldiers wove a crown out of thorns and placed it on his head, and clothed him in a purple robe, and they came to him and said, "Hail, King of the Jews!" —JOHN 19:2-3

The soldiers hurt Jesus very much, but he suffered all this in silence. Jesus knew that someday his kingdom would come. He did not strike back at those who hurt him, but offered his suffering up for them and for all people.

Dear Mother Mary, help me let Jesus love others through me.

JESUS CARRIES THE CROSS

So they took Jesus, and carrying the cross by himself, he went out to what is called the Place of the Skull, which is called in Hebrew, Golgotha. —JOHN 19:16-17

Although Jesus was innocent, he took up his cross and carried it up the hill of Calvary. On the way the soldiers beat him, and he fell under the cross. Jesus suffered for us, and gives us the strength to follow him.

Dear Mary, you were very sad when you saw your son carrying the cross. When He saw you He felt stronger. Help me assist others who may be hurting.

JESUS DIES ON THE CROSS

After they had crucified him, they divided his garments by casting lots; then they sat down and kept watch over him there. —MATTHEW 27:35-36

As he hung on the cross, Jesus forgave his enemies. He gave us Mary to be our Mother, and gave us to Mary as her children. When everything was finished, Jesus bowed his head and died.

Dear Mother Mary, you were heartbroken when Jesus died, but you knew He did it for us. Thank you for sharing your Son with us all.

THE GLORIOUS MYSTERIES

Sunday, Wednesday

THE RESURRECTION OF JESUS

Then the angel said to the women in reply, "Do not be afraid! I know that you are seeking Jesus the crucified. He is not here, for he has been raised just as he said. Come and see the place where he lay." —MATTHEW 28:5-6

After three days, Jesus arose from the dead! He won! He did it for us, so we could share in His victory over sin and death. Alleluia!

Dear Mother Mary, thank you for giving us your Son Jesus, who rose from the dead so we could always be with Him.

THE ASCENSION OF JESUS

As he blessed them, he parted from them and was taken up to heaven. —LUKE 24:51

Forty days after His Resurrection, Jesus gathered His disciples together. He told them to wait in Jerusalem until they received power from heaven. After Jesus blessed them, He was taken up into heaven.

Dear Mother Mary, help us to stay close to Jesus and bring His love to everyone.

THE DESCENT OF THE HOLY SPIRIT

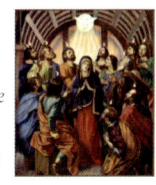

When the time for Pentecost was fulfilled ... suddenly there came from the sky a noise like a strong driving wind, and it filled the entire house in which they were. ... And they were all filled with the holy Spirit. —ACTS 2:1-4

On Pentecost, the Holy Spirit filled the disciples with faith and courage to bring God's love and forgiveness to all people.

Dear Mother Mary, you are filled with the Holy Spirit. Please pray that the Spirit will fill me with His fire of love. Amen.

THE ASSUMPTION OF MARY

Mary said: "My soul proclaims the greatness of the Lord; / and my spirit rejoices in God my savior. / ...The Mighty One has done great things for me, / and holy is his name."
—LUKE 1:46-47, 49

Mary always said 'Yes' to God. God gave Mary a special gift at the end of her life. Jesus took His Mother, body and soul, to be in heaven with Him, forever.

Dear Mother Mary, please help me to love God that I may live forever with Him. Amen.

THE CROWNING OF MARY

"He has helped his servant Israel, / remembering his mercy."
—LUKE 1:54-55

Adam and Eve disobeyed God, and lost His grace. Mary obeyed God, and through Jesus we have received God's grace back into our souls. Mary is our Heavenly Mother. She is very powerful and is always able to help us when we call on her.

Dear Mother Mary, please wrap us in your arms of love that we may always be close to God and bring others to rejoice in His salvation. In Jesus' name. Amen!

A FATHER'S PRAYERS

Consecration to the Hearts of Jesus and Mary

Most Sacred Heart of Jesus and Immaculate Heart of Mary, I consecrate myself and my whole family to you. We consecrate to you all that we are, all that we have, and all that we love. To you we give our bodies, our hearts, our souls, our home, and our country. Mindful of this consecration, we now purpose to follow You, Lord Jesus, without regard for human respect. O most Sacred Heart of Jesus and Immaculate Heart of Mary, accept our humble confidence and this act of consecration by which we entrust ourselves and all our family to you. In you we put all our hope and we shall never be confounded.

Most Sacred Heart of Jesus, I place my trust in You.
Sweet Heart of Mary, be my salvation.

A House Blessing

God bless the corners of this house,
And be the lintel blest;
And bless the hearth and bless the board,
And bless each place of rest;
And bless each door that opens wide
To stranger as to kin;
And bless each crystal windowpane
That lets the starlight in;
And bless the rooftree overhead
And every sturdy wall;
The peace of man, the peace of God,
The peace of love on all.

Prayer for Our Marriage

Heavenly Father, You brought my wife and me together out of Your great love for us. You call us by our marriage to be a sign of the union of Jesus with His Bride, the Church. You have chosen me from all other men to love and cherish my wife. Help me to do so with Your tenderness, love, and loyalty.

Grant that my wife and I may have a true and understanding love for each other. Grant that we may both be filled with faith and trust. Give us the grace to live with each other in peace and harmony. May we always bear with one another's weaknesses and grow from each other's strengths. Help us to forgive one another's failings. Grant us patience, kindness, cheerfulness, and the willingness to place each other's well-being ahead of our own.

May the love that brought us together grow and mature with each passing year. Bring us both ever closer to You through our love for each other. Let our love grow to perfection. Thank You, Lord, for the gift of our marriage. In Jesus' name, we pray. Amen.

> *"So they are no longer two, but one flesh.*
> *Therefore, what God has joined together,*
> *no human being must separate."*
>
> —MATTHEW 19:6

Prayer to Conceive

Dear Mother Mary and good Saint Joseph, you received from God the treasured blessing of divine parenthood. In the name of the joys you knew when you nurtured your beloved Baby, please hear and bless my petition! With Jesus you make up the Holy Family, and you hold parenthood very dear. You know the great privilege of bringing into this world a new soul destined to praise God forever in heaven. Dear Joseph and Mary, I ask that through your intercession God would grant to my wife and me the grace to conceive a child.

Heavenly Father, for You all things are possible. In Your Word You tell us:

Children too are a gift from the LORD,
the fruit of the womb, His reward.

—Psalm 127:3

O Father, I trust in You and in Your unconditional love for us. I believe that You will hear my prayer, offered through the intercession of Saint Joseph and Mother Mary, Jesus' parents on earth. I believe that You will answer me according to Your Divine Will, for You have promised to give us the desires of our heart as we delight in You. O Lord, increase in us always Your presence and power. Thank You for Your mercy, grace, peace, and provision. In Jesus' name. Amen.

Jesus, Mary, and Joseph, I place my trust in you!

Thanksgiving for Conceiving

Dear Heavenly Father, thank You from the bottom of my heart for allowing my wife and me to conceive a new life! We rejoice in this precious gift, O Lord. You are the Father of all life, and all good gifts come to us from You, especially the gift of human life, the gift of another soul created to share eternity with You.

Dear Saint Joseph and Mother Mary, thank you for hearing and blessing our petition! Please bring our gratitude to our Heavenly Father, Who has manifested His power and glory within us by creating another human soul to be cared for, nurtured, and loved. In like manner, Joseph and Mary, bring our gratitude to your Son, Our Lord Jesus Christ, Who has revealed His eternal wisdom inside us by fashioning in silence a soul destined to live forever.

Dear Holy Spirit, thank You for magnifying Your everlasting love to us by fashioning in my wife a precious, unrepeatable, human being! May Your breath of life fill our child in preparation for the Sacrament of Baptism yet to come.

Dear Saint Joseph and Mother Mary, you have obtained this wonderful grace for us by your intercession. Please accept our sincere thanks and gratitude. Please join your prayer to ours and bring them before the Lord of all life. Amen.

Prayer for a Happy Delivery

Dear Mother Mary, in the fullness of time you gave birth to a Son, destined to redeem the entire human race. My wife too, will soon give birth, and I ask your prayer that God will grant her a safe and happy delivery.

Dear Heavenly Father, please watch over our unborn child in the final stages of gestation, and grant that it will be positioned correctly for a safe and healthy birth. May our child receive all the nourishment it needs as it is preparing to enter the world. I also pray for those who will help my wife deliver our baby—the health professionals who will attend her, the family and friends who will support us. Thank You for their concern and support as together we prepare to bring this new life into the world. Bless them all, Lord, in Your Divine mercy, and grant that all will be well.

Dear Saint Gerard, patron of mothers, God blessed you with wonderful gifts of help and healing. I also ask your intercession that my wife might have a safe and successful delivery.

Good Saint Joseph, Safeguard of Families, and dear Mother Mary, Our Lady of Happy Delivery, pray for us who have recourse to thee!

Prayer is a great weapon, a rich treasure, a wealth that is never exhausted, an undisturbed refuge, a cause of tranquility, the root of a multitude of blessings and their source.

—SAINT JOHN CHRYSOSTOM

Prayer for My Wife After Childbirth

Dear Heavenly Father, thank You and praise You today for the safe delivery of our new baby! Thank You also for my wife, and for this awesome opportunity You have given us to participate with You in the creation and delivery of a new life.

Dear Lord, through the intercession of Mary, Your Mother, and Saint Joseph, Your foster father, I ask You now to send forth Your healing grace and peace upon my wife as she recuperates after our child's birth. Grant rest to her soul and renewing strength and vigor to her body.

Dear Mother Mary, you cared for your Infant Son, and you know the need of a child for a mother's warm care and tender love. Please intercede with your Divine Son for my wife and grant that she may obtain a complete restoration through the merciful compassion of the Most High.

Dear God, please strengthen my family and me that we may care for my wife and our new baby in the joy of the Lord. Grant us the patience and goodness that flows from Your Holy Spirit and makes for a truly happy family. In Jesus' name. Amen.

Mary, Mother of Jesus, be our Mother as well!

Blessing of an Infant

Dear Lord Jesus Christ, Son of the living God, You were begotten before time began, yet You chose to become one of us, and to be born as an infant. You love the innocence of childhood, which You showed by tenderly embracing and blessing the little ones brought to You. Please bless this child as he/she journeys through life, and let no evil ways corrupt his/her soul. May this little one advance in wisdom, age, and grace, and be pleasing to You who are God, living and reigning with the Father, in the unity of the Holy Spirit, forever and ever. Amen.

Blessing of a Child

Dear Lord Jesus Christ, You said: "Let the little children come to me, and do not stop them, for the kingdom of God belongs to such as these." We ask You, Lord, to pour out the power of your Holy Spirit on our child by virtue of the faith and devotion of Your Church and of our faith as well. May *(name)* advance in wisdom and virtue before God and men, may he/she reach a blessed old age, and may he/she finally attain everlasting salvation in heaven with all our family. We ask this of You Who lives and reigns forever and ever. Amen.

Blessing of a Family

O Heavenly Father, we thank and praise You for establishing the human family, based on Your own family of Father, Son, and Holy Spirit. The family is the domestic church and our first school of faith. Bless our family, and keep us united in spirit, that we may love one another and work together to bring about Your Will on the earth.

May the Holy Family of Nazareth be our model, with Mary and Joseph as our example, and the Child Jesus as our inspiration. Help us pray, work, and play together. In Jesus' name we pray. Amen.

Family Prayer

God made us a family.
We need one another.
We love one another.
We forgive one another.
We work together.
We play together.
We worship together.
Together we learn God's Word.
Together we grow in Christ.
Together we love all people.
Together we serve our God.
Together we hope for Heaven.
There are our hopes.
Help us obtain them, Father,
through Jesus your Son,
Our Lord. Amen.

Prayer For a Handicapped Child

Dear God, You are truly our Father—the Father of Mercies and the God of all Consolation. You have chosen the weak things of the world to confound the strong.

O God, You have seen fit in Your plan of salvation that my child should labor under a difficulty which others do not have. It is difficult, O Lord, to see my child endure this handicap, yet this limitation draws my child closer to my heart than ever, and reminds me that I, too, am powerless without You.

O Lord, please bless *(name)* with Your grace and peace. I pray that You would heal and restore him/her, according to Your Will. Even so, Father, I accept that You may choose to bring complete healing only in eternity, when all shall be made new.

Father, I pray for the grace to love my child and even to embrace his/her handicap, which You have allowed for Your own purposes. Fill my child, the light of my eyes, with Your presence, and in his/her weakness may Your power be made perfect. Thank You for the gift of *(name)* to our family. May You receive all the glory and the praise through *(name)* as well.

Dear Blessed Mother Mary, you had unique challenges in raising God's only Son, but God always gave you the grace to accomplish His perfect Will. Please help me to love and cherish my child and raise him/her as best I can to become a vibrant witness to God's unconditional love. Amen.

Prayer For a Sick Child

Dear Jesus, my Lord and Savior, I turn with confidence to You today. You know how parents suffer when one of their children is ill. Please lay Your healing hands through the power of the Holy Spirit upon *(name)*. Send forth Your healing grace, Lord Jesus, and bring him/her Your mercy and peace.

Dear Mother Mary, you are the Consoler of the Afflicted and the Health of the Sick. Today I come to you on behalf of my child who is sick and in need of God's healing power. I believe, yet I also feel sometimes helpless to do anything, and I admit I am powerless to restore my child quickly to health.

I call upon you, my gracious and dearest Mother and Mother of my child. Through your intercession, God blessed my child in the womb and at birth; please bless with Him my child now, and restore him/her to health. I consecrate *(name)*—body, soul, and spirit—to you, my dear Mother. Since *(name)* is your own, guard him/her and keep him/her as your property and possession. I ask this through Jesus Christ Our Lord, Amen.

O Mary Help of Christians, pray for us.
Our Lady of Lourdes, pray for us.
Good Saint Joseph, pray for us.

Prayer for a Growing Infant

Mother Most Admirable, Mother of the Infant Jesus, our little baby is growing rapidly, gaining weight, and changing daily. Thank you for your watchful care and intercession for *(name)* before God. Please continue to nurture him/her with the special graces and blessings that flow through you.

Dear Heavenly Father, please give *(name)* strong limbs and a healthy body. Watch over him/her whether awake or asleep, that he/she may grow in wisdom, age, and grace before God and man. In Jesus' name we pray. Amen.

Prayer for My Children

Dear Saint Joseph and Mother Mary, in your parenthood of Jesus you have become Foster-Father and Mother of us all. Praise God for this great gift to us!

Today I place my children again under your true and loving care. Please protect and watch over them with your fatherly and motherly compassion. Bless their spirits, that they may come to know, love, and serve the Lord. Guard their minds to be ever pure and focused on the true, the good, and the beautiful.

Dear Joseph and Mary, in the Scripture it is written: "A joyful heart is health for the body." (Proverbs 17:22) Please guard my children's hearts that they will be obedient to the Lord and so will be content, joyful, and true. Bless their bodies with health and strength. Preserve in their souls the image of God they received in Baptism. May they grow to their full potential. Always, Joseph and Mary, protect them, preserve them, and watch over them in your paternal and maternal care.

Finally, dear Joseph and Mary, please help me also to be a good husband to my wife and a good father to our children. Please supply where we may be lacking, and protect our children from all evil. We ask all this of God our Father, through your intercession, in Jesus' name. Amen.

Good Saint Joseph, Pray for us!
Queen of the Most Holy Family, Pray for us!
Jesus, Mary, and Joseph, I love you; save souls.

Child Correction

The proper correction of a child is one of the primary responsibilities of a parent. "Train up a child in a way he should go; even when he is old, he will not swerve from it." (PROVERBS 22:6) Even so, unless it is done in love, discipline can wound and even break a child's spirit.

God has chosen *you* from all eternity to raise and nurture your children. Since your discipline will affect your child's character for the rest of his or her life, it is very important to carry out this responsibility wisely and appropriately.

Your child needs positive eye contact, physical affection, focused attention (one on one time), and appropriate discipline from you. The key to your child's heart is to stay in touch with him or her and to not allow a wounded spirit to develop. Obedience is the great virtue of childhood, as Jesus showed us: "He went down with them and came to Nazareth, and was obedient to them." (LUKE 2:51) Insist on obedience and respect from your children, and treat them with proper dignity in return.

It is a mistake to correct a child, or even worse, to strike a child, out of anger. When you need to discipline, do so with self-control and dignity, and your child will be far more likely to respond.

Only God can give you the patience, wisdom, and courage to discipline your child properly and lovingly. A moment of prayer or deliberation can defuse a fearful or angry temper and give you the grace to administer a prudent and profitable discipline.

If you do fail, ask forgiveness and try again. Be encouraged! God is more concerned about your child's development than you are, and He will help you!

For the Grace to Properly Correct a Child

Dear Heavenly Father, all authority comes from You. In giving my wife and me the gift of parenthood, You have also conferred on us the holy and serious responsibility of not provoking our children to anger, but of bringing them up in Your training and instruction.

Help me not to shirk this duty, but to fulfill it according to Your will. May I always remember that in giving correction I stand in Your place. Help me to discipline in a calm, fatherly manner, with a firm but caring hand.

Help me remember to pray before I discipline. May my child actually draw nearer to me through appropriate discipline, and grow into the person You have created him/her to be. Dear Saint Joseph, please help me, a father like you, to lovingly guide and discipline my children. In Jesus' name. Amen.

For a True Spirit of Fatherhood

Dear God, I rejoice in the gift of this beautiful child You have given to my wife and me. Grant that *(name)* may teach me the ways of God. When I see his/her eyes, I am reminded of the innocence of Jesus. May my child's ready smile remind me of Your great and unconditional love that is always there for me. May the helplessness and vulnerability of my child remind me that I too am a little child in Your eyes.

Dear Heavenly Father, may my child's first attempts to speak help me remember Your Wisdom which spoke the universe into being. May my child's complete trust in me lead me to put my total trust in You.

Dear God, my child and I already share a deep affection and bonding. Help me to deepen my own love for You, my Heavenly Father, a Father Who cares for me, Who provides for me, Who protects me, and Who is leading me to eternal life. O my God, I believe in You, I hope in You, I adore You, and I love You. Have mercy on all parents and grant us a true spirit of fatherhood and motherhood to help us love and cherish the children You have so generously given us.

Dear God, You have given so much to me. I ask Your power and anointing to be the best father I can be for my child, through the intercession of Mary, My Queen and my Mother, and Saint Joseph, her most chaste spouse. In Jesus' name. Amen.

Prayer for Strength

Dear Heavenly Father, Your Word tells me: "They that wait upon the Lord shall renew their strength," (ISAIAH 40:31) and "I can do all things through Christ who strengthens me." (PHILIPPIANS 4:13)

I need Your strength today, O Lord. I ask You to fill me now with Your presence and power, to strengthen me for the work I have to do and for all that lies before me. I love my wife and children very much and I beg Your help to fulfill my vocation as husband and father. Some days I feel overwhelmed and worn down, and it is then that I need Your powerful aid, O Lord.

Dear Saint Joseph, patron of fathers, and Mary, Help of Christians, your intercession with God is powerful, for you were Jesus' parents on earth. Your love for me is tender and true, for you are my Foster-Father and my Mother as well. Confidently then I come to you to seek your aid and protection. In my calling as a dad, I beg your help, dearest Joseph and Mary. I call on you for your special assistence in guarding and directing each soul that God has given me. In every sorrow, I confide in you. Please pray I will have strength to bear cheerfully and victoriously the challenges of each day.

Dear God, help me to live the present with joy and to face the future without regrets. May my thoughts, words, and deeds bring You joy, glory, and praise. In Jesus' name. Amen.

Prayer After a Miscarriage

Dear Heavenly Father, I come before You today with a heavy heart. My wife and I have lost the child from within her womb, the child You gave us, O Lord! I do not want to accept this, yet I bring my sorrow to you, O compassionate Father, because You understand. We are filled with a deep sadness, and feel alone, although our family and friends do their best to comfort us. We trust in You, even though we do not understand.

O Father, You know what is best for us always. Perhaps our child would have suffered greatly in life, or wasn't ready yet to come into the world. We ask you, dear God, to please send Your mercy on all parents who are experiencing the loss and pain of a miscarriage, and console them with the sure certainty that they will see their little treasure again.

I admit I feel some fear for the future, an apprehension that this could happen again. Nevertheless, O Lord, I put my trust in You. You are the God Who heals us; You are the Good Shepherd Who will neither leave us nor forsake us, so we are at peace. Please kiss our little angel, and tell him/her that we yearn for the day we will be together again, with You, in the Kingdom of heaven.

O Lord, grant my wife and me the grace to conceive again, according to Your will. Help us continue to make our home a welcoming place for all life. We ask this in the name of Jesus, Comforter of all who mourn, in Whom we put our trust. Amen.

Prayer at the Death of a Child

Dear Heavenly Father, our child is gone, and what can we say? We feel so lonely, so sad; we miss our child so very much. We just want to run into Your arms and Your consoling embrace. We need Your comfort, dear God. We have lost our child, the light of our eyes, just as You suffered the death of your Son, Jesus, when He gave His life on the cross for us.

O dear Saint Joseph and most compassionate Mother Mary, I don't understand why God has allowed this sorrow to come into our lives. However, we trust Him as our loving Father Who knows what is best for us. O dear Foster-Father and Mother, please take our child now into your arms, and hold him/her close to your hearts. Please pray that God will give my family and me His grace and strength to carry on. Through your prayers may we be faithful to the end. In Jesus' name. Amen.

Prayer to a Child in Heaven

My dear *(name)*, you are no longer with us here on earth. Your Mom and I miss you very much and we long to see you. Still, we believe that you are now with Jesus, Mother Mary, Saint Joseph, and all the angels and saints. It is hard for us to understand why you were taken from our arms, but you can never be taken from our hearts. We love you and will love you forever, until time is no more. Please pray for us, dear *(name)* that we may be faithful to our duties here below and thereby come to hold you someday in our waiting arms. Amen.

Dedication of a Family to Mary

Most Blessed Virgin Mary, Immaculate Queen and Mother, the refuge and consolation of all troubled souls! I kneel here before you with my family and choose you for my Lady, Mother, and Advocate with God.

I dedicate myself and all who belong to me to your service forever. I beg you, O Mother of God, to receive us into the company of your servants. Take us under your protection. Help us in life and at the hour of our death.

Mother of Mercy, I name you Lady and Queen of my family and relatives, my interests and all my undertakings. Take charge of them; dispose of everything as it pleases you.

Bless me and all my family. Never let any of us offend your Son. In every temptation defend us; protect us in every danger; provide for us in the necessities of life; counsel us in doubt; comfort us in every sorrow, in every sickness, and especially in the final sorrow of death.

Never let the powers of Hell boast that they have enslaved any of those who here consecrate themselves to you. Grant that we may all enter into Heaven to thank you, and in your company, to praise and love Jesus our Redeemer for all eternity. Amen.

—Saint Alphonsus Liguori

Thanksgiving for a Happy Family

Dear Heavenly Father, thank You for the gift of a happy family! Thank You for all the many blessings You have generously given to our family, through the love and prayers of our Blessed Mother Mary. Thank You, Father, for the gift of our marriage. Thank You for blessing our marriage with the gift of children and parenthood.

Thank You for protecting us from all evils that might have befallen us. Thank you for providing for our needs and so many of our wants as well. We are grateful, dear God, for the healings You have granted our family and the many times You have revived us and kept us from sickness and disease.

Father, thank You for consoling us in our times of sorrow, with Your rod and Your staff that give us comfort. Thank You also for Your sustaining hand when trials have threatened to overwhelm us. Thank You for all the family, friends, and supporters with which You have surrounded us. Thank You for the many joys and times of togetherness we have shared as a family. Most of all, O Lord, thank You for the gift of faith, which unites us to You, our Blessed Mother, and all believers.

O Mary, Mother of God, we put ourselves and our future into your hands. Please present our family to God Most High, and ask His continued Fatherly assistance with us all the days of our lives and at the hour of our death. In Jesus' name. Amen.

For Protection of the Family

Dear Heavenly Father, I thank You and praise You for the gift of my family. You have called us from all eternity to be members of one particular family, sharing our lives and hearts together daily.

O Lord, You committed the care of Your only Son to Our Blessed Mother and Saint Joseph amid the many dangers of this world. Through their intercession, we ask You today to grant Your special protection to our family.

Protect us in spirit, soul, and body, O God. Grant that we might come to know the true, to taste the good, and to see the beautiful, always according to Your Will. Help us always to walk in the way You set before us. Merciful Father, please fill our hearts with the love of Jesus. Continue to keep us all in good health, growing in wisdom, age, and grace before You and all people.

Dear Mother Mary, Morning Star and Help of Christians, we beg your powerful protection as well. Keep us all close to you and your Divine Son.

Virgin Most Powerful, pray for us!

In Jesus' name. Amen.

For True Family Prosperity

O Eternal Father, thank You for the gift of our family. Your Word tells us, "I know the plans I have for you," says the Lord, "plans to prosper you and not to harm you; plans to give you a future full of hope." (JEREMIAH 29:11) I pray for every member of my family, O Lord, that You would fulfill Your plans for us.

Dear God, You have gifted each of us with distinct talents, abilities, and attributes, that we might share Your love with the world in a unique and unrepeatable way. You want us to grow and prosper, to be mature persons, strong in all You call us to be. You want us to bring hope, joy, and peace to our world.

O Father, through the prayers of our Blessed Mother, help us to choose the way that is right and so come to fulfill Your perfect Will for us. In Your embrace may we 'know ourselves to be loved,' and go forth to love and serve You and our neighbor.

Dear Mother Mary, may we as a family be a blessing to others, as were Abraham and Sarah to their visitors. Help us to be always hospitable and welcoming, receiving others and sharing with them as we would with the Lord Himself. In this way, when our life is done and we meet the Lord, may He be pleased with us and allow us to enter into heaven, where the celebrating never ceases. Amen.

The children of your servants shall continue,
and their posterity shall be established before you.
—PSALM 102:28

For the Grace to be Faithful to Our Marriage

Dear God, thank You for the gift of our marriage! You have called my wife and me to be one flesh. In our marital union we are a sign of Your love for Your Bride, the Church. Thank You for bringing my wife into my life, and for giving her to be my friend, my helper, the life of my heart, and the mother of our children.

Lord Jesus, at the Wedding of Cana You honored marriage and raised it to the dignity of a sacrament—and You are present at every marriage. Please grant that my wife and I will be ever faithful to our wedding vows. May we always keep ourselves for one another, and grow more in love with each passing day.

O Jesus, on the cross You appeared weak and foolish, yet in truth You were the power and wisdom of God. Help us to remember Your cross when we encounter difficulties and setbacks in our marriage. Help us die to ourselves, when necessary, so that our marriage might live in You. Finally, may we be kind to one another.

Thank you for the children with which You have blessed us. In our union may we always be open to the gift of new life. Thank You for the family and friends You have sent to stand with us in joy and sorrow. Dear Mother Mary, intercede with Your Son for our marriage, that we might live a life pleasing to Him. We ask all this through Christ Jesus Our Lord. Amen.

For a Child in Moral Danger

Dear Heavenly Father, You are the Holy One. You created all of us to live forever in heaven, a place of joy and eternal bliss, a place where we will ever be with You, the angels, and the saints.

You also created us with a free will to choose or reject You. Through the devil, sin came into the world and now we struggle daily to reject the evil and choose the good. However, in Christ You have overcome all the power of the enemy.

Furthermore, You have given us Mary, our Immaculate Mother, and Saint Michael the Archangel as our special helpers in our battle with the powers of darkness. O Mother Mary, please protect my child in the present danger he/she faces. You know how greatly sin offends God, and therefore you abhor sin and its consequences. You saw Your Son suffer His Passion and Death to redeem us from sin and free us from its hold on us.

O Mother, defend my children from the dangers of sin and from the attack of the enemy. Go, I pray, to the side of my child and show yourself a Mother! Should my child fall, intercede with God that he/she will quickly rise and be restored. O Mary, since heaven is our true home, please pray that we will all together enter the kingdom and there share eternal joy forever! Amen.

Virgin most powerful, pray for us.

Jesus, Mary, and Joseph, I love you; save souls.

For a Wayward Son

Dear Heavenly Father, I come to you today to share a deep burden—my son has wandered from You and the path of righteousness. Dear God, You know my love for my son, how overjoyed my wife and I were to hear we had conceived, how proud we were when he was born, how we have raised him and taught him as best we could. As a child, his heart was wide open to wonder, faith, and love.

Dear Mother Mary, your love for our son surpasses even our own, for you know the price that Jesus paid for his salvation. Please, O Mother, pray and intercede for *(name)*, that he will come to his senses and return to his Father's house.

Dear Lord Jesus, through the prayers of your Mother Mary and good Saint Joseph, send out Your grace and light upon my son. Please cause believers to cross his path who will remind him of You and Your faithful love. Touch his heart with Your mercy and help him to turn his heart towards home. I especially ask the intercession of Saint Monica, who prayed over thirty years for her son, Augustine. Upon his conversion, Saint Augustine became one of the greatest lights in the Church, for with God, nothing shall be impossible. In confidence, then, I ask this favor in Your name, Lord Jesus. Amen.

> *"I have not come to call the righteous to repentance but sinners."*
>
> —LUKE 5:32

For a Wayward Daughter

Dear God, our lovely daughter has strayed from You and Your way. However, she can never stray from Your unconditional love for her, mirrored in Mother Mary and her maternal care for each one of Your children. Therefore, O Lord, reach out and touch our daughter's heart and awaken there a love for Mary and for the womanhood shining in her. Guide her way and help her return to that which is holy, true, and good.

Dear Mother Mary, you are "our tainted nature's solitary boast." You are the glory of women and of all that is good and true in woman. You want to see the beauty and strength of your own womanhood reflected in all of your daughters. Please wrap your mantle of protection around (name), safeguard her from the enemy's designs, and embrace her tenderly for me.

O Mother Mary, I miss the spiritual communion my daughter and I used to share. She is a good girl and needs your protection and provision now more than ever. I commend (name) now to you, Mother Mary, and pray that God will soon restore her to a holy, virtuous, and joyful life.

Dear Lord Jesus, You were compassionate towards sinners and sought to guide them to Yourself. In Your mercy, Good Shepherd, recover my daughter and return her to Your fold. Protect her through Your Precious Blood. I pray all this in Your name, Lord Jesus, and for Your sake. Amen.

Virgin most powerful, pray for us.

For a Son or Daughter Considering Marriage

Dear Heavenly Father, our son/daughter would like to get married someday, and I come to ask Your guidance. Please help *(name)* to find his/her vocation in life. If it is to marry, please help them in their choice of a lifetime spouse.

Please help my child to look beyond outward glamor, appearance, and external attractions for the character beneath, the depth of the spirit, that tells the true nature of the other. Help this future spouse to first be a good friend to my child, that together they may grow into the couple You call them to be.

Dear God, help *(name)* choose, if possible, a fervent Catholic Christian as a mate. May his/her future spouse be someone who loves You, Lord, and seeks to follow You in his/her life.

Dear Saint Joseph and Mother Mary, I ask your intercession before God for *(name)*. In honor of your courtship and marriage, please help him/her to choose the right partner, and may they both fulfill all God's plans for them. May they truly enjoy one another and find in each other a true friend. In Jesus' name. Amen.

For a Married Son or Daughter

Dear Heavenly Father, I praise and thank You for the gift of marriage! You Yourself instituted marriage in the beginning, and through Your Son, You made it a sacrament. Please watch over my son and his wife/my daughter and her husband, and give them Your grace to grow together in love.

Father, may they care for one another and seek to support each other. Help them to communicate together, often and much, and to grow in communion together. According to Your Will, O God, please bless them with children, and may they raise their family to Your honor and glory.

Help me accept this marriage, dear Lord, with all my heart, realizing I am not losing one child but gaining another. May this couple walk together all the days of their lives, and let them be for each other a special treasure, kept for heaven.

Dear Mother Mary, you had compassion on the couple at Cana; look with mercy on this particular couple as well. Intercede with them before the Father, that they will always keep Christ at the center of their lives. May they grow in Faith, Hope, and Love all the days of their life. In Jesus' name. Amen.

Therefore they are no longer two, but one flesh.
What therefore God has joined together, let no one take apart.

—Matthew 19:6

Prayer for Healing

O Heavenly Father, God of Love, You gave us Your Son Jesus to be Physician of our souls and Healer of our bodies and minds as well. Lord Jesus, I turn to You in this time of illness. Please come to me and lay Your healing hands on me. Let the warmth, peace, and healing power of Your Spirit fill me now with Your life and love. I receive You, Lord Jesus!

Heal me according to Your Divine Will, O Lord, and enable me to serve You and my family with a healthy body, soul, and spirit. May Your joy be my strength this day and all the days of my life. Saint Joseph, Hope of the Sick, pray for us. Amen.

Prayer for a Sick Wife

O Heavenly Father, You revive and renew Your creation, and bring healing to those who are sick. Most merciful Jesus, You are the consolation and salvation of all who trust in You. Grant my wife recovery of health according to Your Divine Will, that together we might praise and magnify Your Holy Name. Fill her with Your light and love, and grant her consolation in her hour of illness. Please come to her now, and lay Your healing hands on her. Let the warmth, peace, and healing power of Your Spirit fill her to overflowing.

Through the intercession of Mary, Health of the Sick, renew my wife's body and refresh her soul. We ask this in Your name, Lord Jesus, through Your death and Resurrection. Amen.

Prayer for a Deceased Wife

O God, Merciful Father and God of all consolation, I come to You now on behalf of my deceased wife. Lord, sometimes it is very hard to understand Your ways and to accept Your will. Still, I trust in You, my Father. Today I give to You the soul of my deceased wife, and I beg You to bring her into Your bosom. She is Your child, O Father; have mercy on her.

Dear Lord Jesus, You are the Resurrection and the Life. Just as Martha and Mary grieved for their brother Lazarus, so I grieve for my wife. Even so, Lord, I place all my trust and hope in You and in Your promise of eternal life. You died to save us, and You are our Mediator with the Father.

Bring my wife into Your presence in the company of the saints. Mercifully grant her Your rest and joy in light of her faithfulness to You and to her vocation. Through the intercession of Mary, may I one day join my wife in the complete bliss of the Beatific Vision. O Mary, look upon *(name)* with pity and please bring her to Paradise, her true home. In Jesus' name I pray. Amen.

Eternal rest grant unto her, O Lord, and let perpetual light shine upon her. May her soul and the souls of all the faithful departed, through the mercy of God, rest in peace. Amen.

Litany of Saint Joseph

V - Lord, have mercy on us.
R - Christ, have mercy on us.
V - Lord, have mercy on us.
V - Christ, hear us.
R - Christ, graciously hear us.
God the Father of Heaven,
R - Have mercy on us.
God the Son, Redeemer of the world,
R - Have mercy on us.
God the Holy Spirit,
R - Have mercy on us.
Holy Trinity, one God,
R - Have mercy on us.

Response: Pray for us.

Holy Mary,
Saint Joseph,
Renowned offspring of David,
Light of Patriarchs,
Spouse of the Mother of God,
Chaste guardian of the Virgin,
Foster father of the Son of God,
Diligent protector of Christ,
Head of the Holy Family,
Joseph most just,
Joseph most chaste,
Joseph most prudent,

Joseph most strong,
Joseph most obedient,
Joseph most faithful,
Mirror of patience,
Lover of poverty,
Model of artisans,
Glory of home life,
Guardian of virgins,
Pillar of families,
Solace of the wretched,
Hope of the sick,
Patron of the dying,
Terror of demons,
Protector of Holy Church,

V - Lamb of God, Who takes away the sins of the world,
R - Spare us, O Lord.
V - Lamb of God, Who takes away the sins of the world,
R - Graciously hear us, O Lord.
V - Lamb of God, Who takes away the sins of the world,
R - Have mercy on us.
V - He made him the lord of his household.
R - And prince over all his possessions.

Let us pray: O God, in Your ineffable providence You were pleased to choose Blessed Joseph to be the spouse of Your most holy Mother; grant, we beg You, that we may be worthy to have him for our intercessor in heaven whom on earth we venerate as our Protector: You who live and reign forever and ever. Amen.

"Of all the people I have known with a true devotion and particular veneration for Saint Joseph, not one has failed to advance in virtue; he helps those who turn to him to make real progress. For several years now, I believe, I have always made some request to him on his feast day, and it has always been granted; and when my request is not quite what it ought to be, he puts it right for my greater benefit."

—Saint Teresa of Avila

NOVENA TO SAINT JOSEPH

Pray the following prayer every day for nine consecutive days. Then, add the appropriate prayer for each day from those on the following pages. You may pray this novena from March 10th to March 19th (Saint Joseph's Feastday) or at any other time.

Novena Prayer to Saint Joseph

This prayer is over 1900 years old. It has never been known to fail.

O Saint Joseph, whose protection is so great, so strong, so prompt before the Throne of God, I place in you all my interests and desires.

O Saint Joseph, do assist me by your powerful intercession and obtain for me from your Divine Son all spiritual blessings through Jesus Christ, Our Lord; so that having engaged here below your Heavenly power, I may offer my Thanksgiving and Homage to the most Loving of Fathers.

O Saint Joseph, I never weary contemplating you and Jesus asleep in your arms. I dare not approach while He reposes near your heart. Press Him in my name and kiss His fine Head for me, and ask Him to return the Kiss when I draw my dying breath. Saint Joseph, Patron of departing souls, pray for us. Amen.

Whoever reads this prayer, hears it, or carries it, will never die a sudden death, nor be drowned, nor will poison take effect on them. They will not fall into the hands of the enemy nor be burned in any fire, nor will they be defeated in battle.

NOVENA TO SAINT JOSEPH

Day 1: Foster Father of Jesus

Saint Joseph, you were privileged to share in the mystery of the Incarnation as the chosen father of Jesus, sharing in His support, upbringing, and protection. For this purpose the Heavenly Father gave you the genuine heart of a father—a heart full of love and self-sacrifice. Dear Saint Joseph, help us also to fulfill God's will in our lives by cooperating daily with His graces and blessings as we serve our families. May His Kingdom come! Amen.

Day 2: Virginal Husband of Mary

Saint Joseph, Mary found her edification in your calm, humble, and deep virtue, purity, and sanctity. I beg of you to obtain for me the grace to love Jesus and Mary with all my heart, as you did, and to love my wife with the tenderness and loyalty with which you loved Mary. Amen.

Day 3: Man Chosen by the Blessed Trinity

Saint Joseph, God the Father granted you all the graces and blessings you needed to be His chosen representative on earth. Chosen by the Holy Spirit, you were entirely consecrated to Jesus, offering Him your very life. Good Saint Joseph, please obtain for me the grace to imitate your virtues so that I too may be pleasing to the Heart of God and fulfill His mission for me. Amen.

Day 4: Faithful Servant

Saint Joseph, you sacrificed everything unselfishly, even cheerfully, as the personal servant of Jesus. Saint Joseph, please obtain for me the grace to be a faithful servant of God as well. Help me to share in your obedience, to trust in God's Will, and to be calm in my trials. Help me imitate your generosity in caring for my family, for there can be no greater reward here on earth than the joy and honor of being God's faithful servant. Amen.

Day 5: Patron of the Church

Saint Joseph, God has appointed you as patron of the Catholic Church because you were the father, protector, guide, and support of the Holy Family. Saint Joseph, please obtain for me the grace to live as a worthy member of the Church. Through your powerful intercession may the Church successfully accomplish her mission: God's glory and the salvation of souls! Amen.

Day 6: Patron of Families

Saint Joseph, you lived, moved, and acted in the loving company of Jesus and Mary, and even died in their arms. Jesus fulfilled toward you all the duties of a faithful son, showing you every mark of honor and affection due to a parent, and Mary loved you as a devoted wife. Saint Joseph, please obtain God's blessing upon my own family. Make our home the kingdom of Jesus and Mary — of peace, joy, hope, and love. Amen.

Day 7: Patron of Workers

Saint Joseph, God willed that you and your foster Son should spend your days together working as carpenters. You learned to work in the presence of God, for as Jesus worked He adored His Father and recommended the welfare of the world to Him. Saint Joseph, teach me to work for God and with God in the spirit of humility and prayer, so that I may offer my toil with Jesus for the good of my family, the world, and myself. Amen.

Day 8: Friend in Suffering

Saint Joseph, you endured suffering in the uncertainty regarding Mary's virginity, in the prophecy of Simeon, the flight into Egypt, and the loss of Jesus in the Temple. You bore your suffering silently and cheerfully, knowing well that true love is a crucified love. Teach me to gratefully accept whatever God sends me, trusting in His perfect will. Dear Saint Joseph, I offer my sufferings, works, and trials with Jesus and Mary to the Father, who makes all things work together for the good. Amen.

Day 9: Patron of a Happy Death

Saint Joseph, how fitting it was at your death that Jesus should stand at your bedside with Mary, the sweetness and hope of all mankind! You gave your entire life to their service; at death you enjoyed the consolation of dying in their loving arms. Yours was a merciful judgment, for your foster Son was your Judge, and Mary was your advocate. Dear Saint Joseph, please obtain for us also the grace of a happy death. In Jesus' name. Amen.